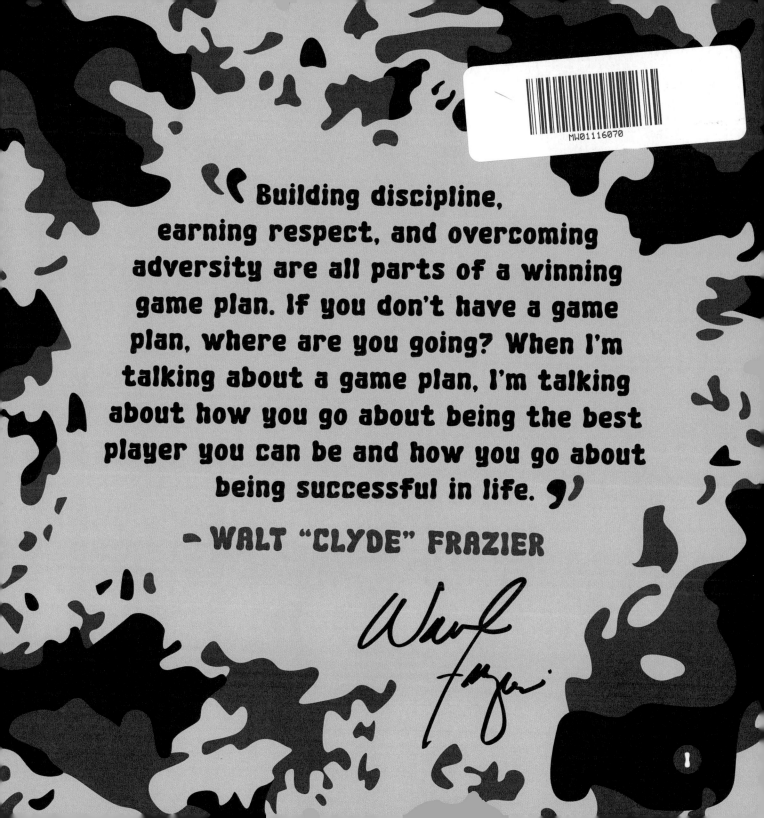

"Building discipline, earning respect, and overcoming adversity are all parts of a winning game plan. If you don't have a game plan, where are you going? When I'm talking about a game plan, I'm talking about how you go about being the best player you can be and how you go about being successful in life."

— WALT "CLYDE" FRAZIER

Winning
&
Grinning
Bounding & Astounding
Stealing & Dealing
THE MECCA
NEW YORK CITY SUBWAY MAP
KNICKS DEFEATED THE LAKERS IN THE 1970 & 1973 N.B.A. FINALS
CHAMPS!
WINNING AND GRINNING
Slamming & Jamming!
Believing &
Dishing & Swishing!
Slicing and Dicing
Swooping & Hooping!
Styling Profiling

IN COLLABORATION WITH

Walt "Clyde" Frazier

Knicks Legend & New York City Icon

WRITTEN & ILLUSTRATED BY
BRIDGET & RYAN SIRGIOVANNI

CREATIVE DIRECTION & ILLUSTRATIONS
BY ELLIOT GERARD OF HEARTLENT GROUP

Book proceeds benefit the
Walt Frazier Youth Foundation.

Walt "Clyde" Frazier

is the GREATEST KNICK OF ALL TIME!

He's a TWO-TIME N.B.A. CHAMPION

He was born in Atlanta,
Georgia as the oldest of nine.
Young Walt was sharing and caring
for his big family all the time.

In high school, he was hustling and muscling as a three-sport star.

Believing and achieving with hard work, he could go real far!

DAVID T. HOWARD
HIGH SCHOOL
CLASS OF 1963

7

1967 NATIONAL INVITATION
TOURNAMENT CHAMPION
& MOST VALUABLE PLAYER

9

Moving and grooving from a small town to N.Y.C. to play for the Knicks under the bright lights at M.S.G.

Clyde

As a rookie, Walt wore a hat with a brim that was wide. It was similar to a character from the movie, Bonnie and Clyde.

& CLYDE

The new Knick was given a new nickname. He was Clyde, he was cool, and what a legend he became!

Slicing and dicing,
bounding and astounding,
Clyde could do it all!

KNICKS DEFEATED THE LAKERS IN THE 1970 & 1973 N.B.A. FINALS

IN 1970, THE KNICKS WON THEIR FIRST N.B.A. TITLE. CLYDE'S PROLIFIC GAME 7 PROVED TO BE VITAL.

SACRIFICE, TEAMWORK AND DEFENSE WERE THE KEY. THE KNICKS BECAME CHAMPS AGAIN IN 1973!

WINNING AND GRINNING

THE KNICKS WERE THE TOAST OF THE TOWN, AND WALT "CLYDE" FRAZIER WAS THE COOLEST GUY AROUND!

(18)

CHAMPS!

1970 GAME 7 : 36 PTS, 19 AST

19

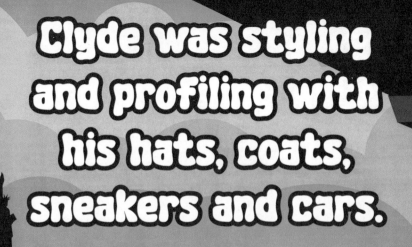

Clyde was styling and profiling with his hats, coats, sneakers and cars.

WALT FRAZIER WAS THE FIRST BASKETBALL PLAYER WITH A SIGNATURE SNEAKER IN 1973!

20

On his plane ride home, he said "sit that trophy next to me!"

CLYDE BOUGHT A PLANE TICKET FOR HIS MVP TROPHY TO TAKE HOME WITH HIM FROM PHOENIX, ARIZONA

1970

ALL-NBA

NBA CHAMPION

YEAR 3

1971

ALL-NBA

YEAR 4

1972

ALL-NBA

YEAR 5

WALT "CLYDE" FRAZIER 10

HE PLAYED 10 SEASONS WITH THE KNICKS

AND IS THE TEAM'S LEADER IN DISHING

10 SEASONS: 1967-77

4791 ASSISTS

1ST ALL-TIME IN TEAM HISTORY

ALL-ROOKIE 1ST TEAM

1968

YEAR 1

ROOKIE YEAR

YEAR 2

1969

1973

ALL-NBA

10

NBA CHAMPION YEAR 6

ALL-NBA

1974

YEAR 7 ★ ★ ★ ★ ★

WALT "CLYDE" FRAZIER **10**

A TRIPLE DOUBLE THREAT WITH HIS BOUNDING AND SWISHING

23 TRIPLE-DOUBLES
1ST ALL-TIME IN TEAM HISTORY

POINTS	ASSISTS	REBOUNDS
14617	4791	4598

1ST ALL-TIME

YEAR 8 — 1975

10

ALL-STAR MVP ★ ★ ★ ★ ★ ★

ALL-NBA

1976

YEAR **9**

★ ★ ★ ★ ☆ ☆ ★ ★

YEAR 10

1977

10

FINAL YEAR

1969-70
WORLD
CHAMPIONS

FRAZIER
10

1972-73
WORLD
CHAMPIONS

In 1979, Clyde's jersey was retired
and raised to the rafters at M.S.G.
The number 10 will forever hang
for all fans to see.

In 1987, Clyde was inducted into the Hoops Hall of Fame.

But, he still had a fire and desire to contribute to the game.

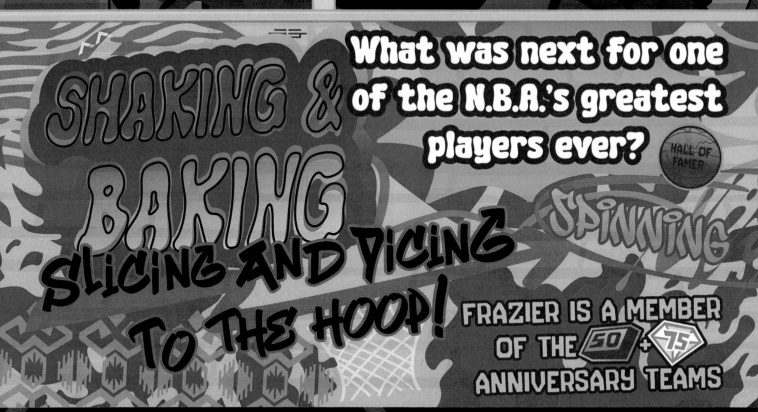

Bouncing to announcing, Clyde started calling games on the radio and then on T.V.

His personality and analysis shines on the network of M.S.G.

KNICKS TAPE

and was awarded as a broadcaster back into the Hall of Fame!

CLYDE & CLYDE

SO NICE IN THE HALL OF FAME TWICE!

WINNING & GRINNING
ELLIOT GERARD

CLYDE IS THE FIRST INDIVIDUAL TO BE INDUCTED AS PLAYER AND ANNOUNCER INTO THE BASKETBALL HALL OF FAME.

Pizzazz

Razzle Dazzle

Clyde has a passion for fashion and loves to design. His custom wardrobe is the coolest of all time.

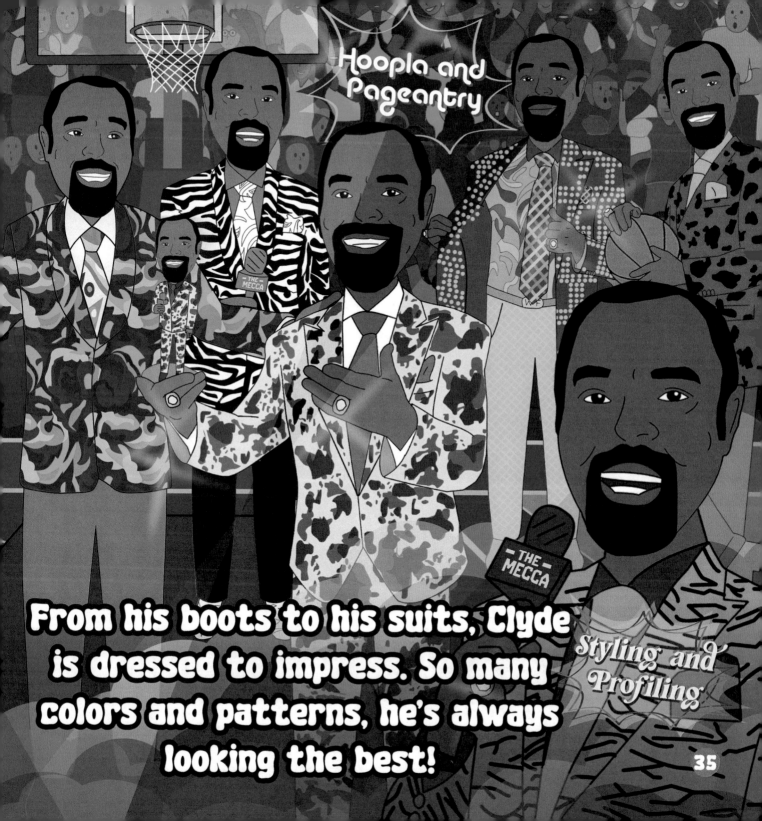

From his boots to his suits, Clyde is dressed to impress. So many colors and patterns, he's always looking the best!

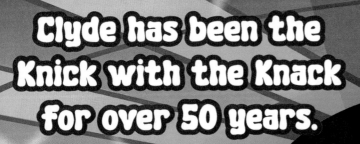

Clyde has been the Knick with the Knack for over 50 years.

THE MECCA OF BASKETBALL

Winning

Grinning

He's beloved by generations of fans for two Hall of Fame careers.

First, a superstar point guard known for his defense and dimes. Then, an iconic announcer known for his suits and his rhymes.

His legacy in New York City is not hard to define.

Walt "Clyde" Frazier

THE GREATEST KNICK OF ALL TIME!

1969-70 WORLD CHAMPIONS

1972-73 WORLD CHAMPIONS

FRAZIER 10

Walt "Clyde" Frazier is THE GREATEST KNICK OF ALL TIME!

CREATIVE DIRECTION AND ILLUSTRATIONS BY

ELLIOT GERARD

OF
HEARTLENT GROUP

Elliot is a life-long Knicks fan who bleeds orange & blue. His love for the team was sparked by the legendary Walt "Clyde" Frazier, whose colorful rhymes and stories captivated Elliot from a young age. Together with his wife Meredith and their children Vivienne & Teddy, they share the excitement of watching games, soaking in every Clyde-ism.

By day, Elliot is the visionary founder of Heartlent Group, a creative agency specializing in sports. With a career spanning 17 years, he's orchestrated over 20 award-winning campaigns for the world's top brands, teams, leagues, and legendary athletes.

Follow Elliot on his journey through sports and creativity @elliotgerard or visit Heartlent.com for more.

WRITTEN AND ILLUSTRATED BY

BRIDGET & RYAN SIRGIOVANNI

Bridget is a Special Education Teacher, working to help children reach their goals. She loves to write and has a degree in Early Childhood Education, Students with Disabilities and a Master's in Literacy.

Ryan works behind-the-scenes in sports TV as part of the Knicks broadcast team on MSG Networks. He has won multiple NY Emmy awards for graphics.

Bridget and Ryan teamed up by combining their skills and passions to create fun and entertaining books for children to enjoy!

They see Clyde as a role model for all and someone who has impacted generations of Knicks fans. They want to share his incredible story with children and basketball fans everywhere!

Discover more books by the authors @BrightTimeBooks

Made in the USA
Middletown, DE
22 August 2024

59597370R00022